paleo eats

REAL FOOD. REAL SIMPLE.

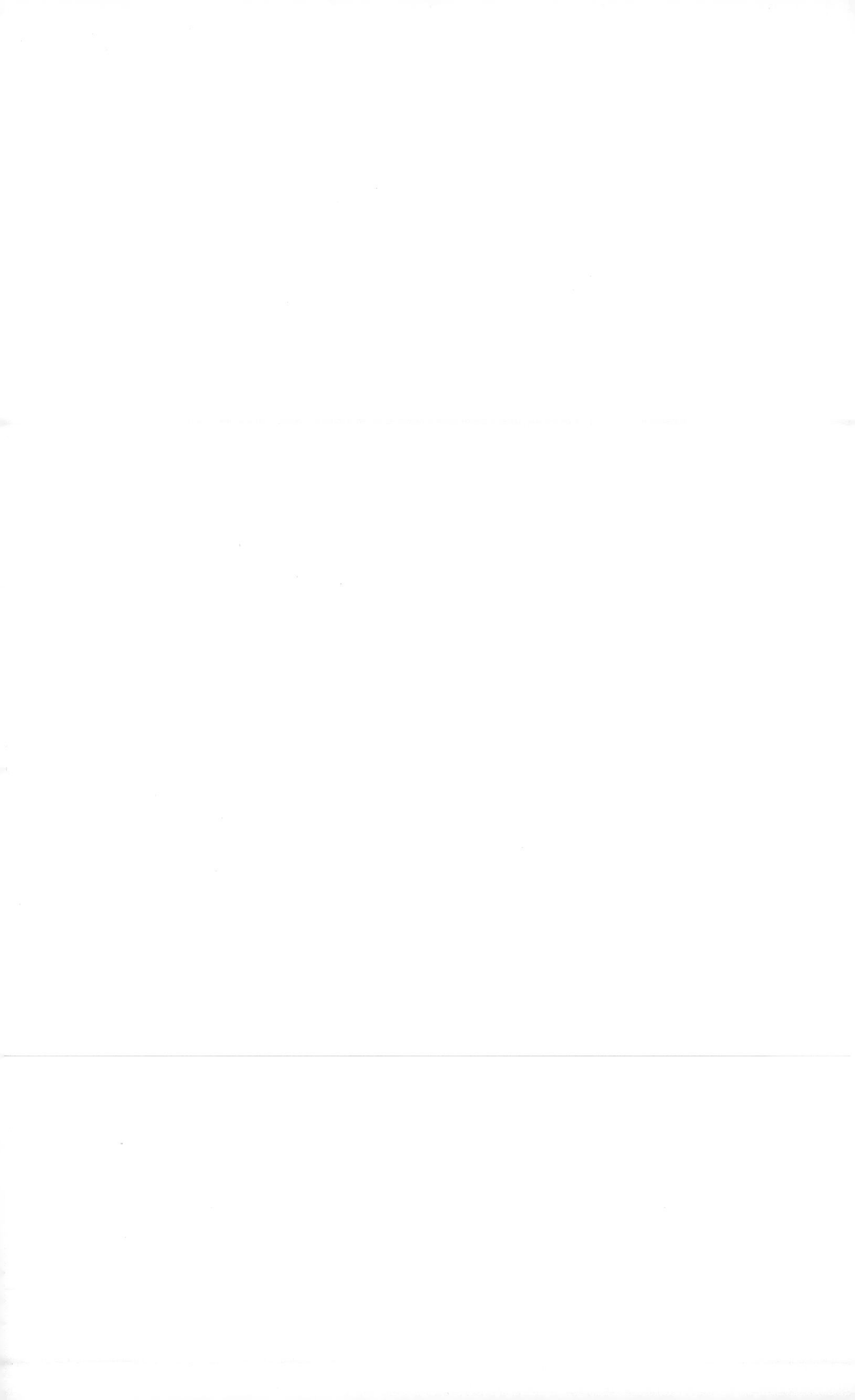

First published in 2015 by Paleohacks, LLC.

Printed in the USA

Design by Allison Dryva

Peaches Photo by Jenn Huls/Shutterstock.com

table of contents

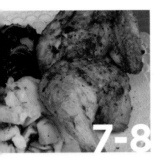

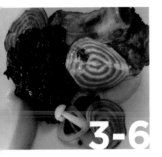

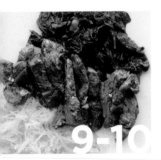

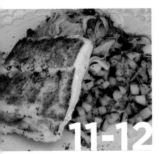

BRAISED PULLED PORK
SAUTÉED KALE
ROASTED BABY CARROTS
WITH GARLIC

CRISPY PORK SHOULDER
ROASTED CAULIFLOWER
SMASHED AND ROASTED
PLANTAINS

BISON SCRAMBLE
SAUTÉED KALE
AND SMASHED TURNIPS

ROASTED VEGETABLE
CHICKEN SOUP
WITH A FRIED EGG

ABOUT PETER SERVOLD

Peter Servold is the owner of Pete's Paleo, a nationally renowned company that produces and ships ready-to-eat Paleo meals around the country.

Peter has worked in the culinary and restaurant field for nearly his whole life, from washing dishes when he was thirteen to running front-of-house operations in multiple restaurants before attending culinary school. After attending Le Cordon Bleu, he worked at Restaurant Eugene in Atlanta, Georgia, where he learned the true meaning of farm-to-table dining: working with the best possible ingredients, from the best local sources.

Today he brings that focus to Pete's Paleo, providing fresh, Paleo-friendly meals to customers across the country.

ABOUT PETE'S PALEO

We started Pete's Paleo to bring fine dining to everyone. Paleo is getting the freshest ingredients, grown and raised properly, from as close a source as possible. Sound familiar? Great food and Paleo are one and the same.

At Pete's Paleo we chase flavor, and nutrition is a bonus. We don't write the menus, our farmers and ranchers do. With a team of chefs to help me, we take whatever vegetables and cuts of meat that come in our kitchen and cook it for our clients, fresh each week. Using the same principles, methods and recipes from my time in fine dining restaurants to bring amazing Paleo food, fresh, to your door.

Life is nuts and we are here to help.

Our kitchen has over 40 years of combined experience at the sous chef level and higher; we scour Southern California for the best stuff, from the coolest farmers and ranchers. Then we take our years of experience and make amazing, delicious, healthy meals that are vacuum sealed for freshness. To enhance flavor, we package them in specially designed shipping containers so that every meal arrives fresh at your door whether you're in Seattle, Las Vegas, Des Moines, NYC or Orlando.

Learn more at PetesPaleo.com and use coupon code: PETESPALEOEATS for 10% off your first order!

ABOUT PALEOHACKS

Paleohacks is one of the largest Paleo communities on the web. We offer everything Paleo, from a Q&A forum where users get their top health questions answered, to our community blog featuring daily recipes, workouts, and wellness content, to our podcast, where we bring in the top experts in the Paleo world to share the latest, cutting edge health information.

We also partner with amazing people (like Pete) to create and publish high-quality informational products and resources to share with the world.

To learn more about Paleohacks, make sure to head on over to http://blog.paleohacks.com/about.

rutabaga purée
pork chop
kale salad
mushrooms

PAN-ROASTED PORK CHOPS PICKLED HON SHIMEJI MUSHROOMS RUTABAGA PURÉE FRIED KALE AND CHIOGGIA BEET AND SHALLOT SALAD

SERVES 4

PORK CHOPS

4 12 oz chops, 1 ½ inches thickness
3 T salt
1 T black peppercorns
1 bay leaf
3 cups water
2 cups ice
1 T avocado oil

Boil salt, pepper and bay leaf in the 3 cups of water for 10 minutes.

Add ice to chill down mixture and then cover pork chops with brine for 24 hours.

Remove from brine and pat dry, let rest at room temp for 30 minutes before cooking. Turn oven on to 400 °F to cook chops and get a large cast iron hot over medium-high heat. Lightly season the chops before they go in the pan with salt and pepper. Remember, they have already been brined, so just a sprinkle on each side.

Add avocado oil to cast iron and sear the chops for three to 4 minutes per side. I like to do two chops at a time so the pan stays hot. If you try to put all the chops in at once it will just steam them and you will not get a good sear. Transfer the seared chops to a sheet tray and place in oven for 6-7 minutes to get a perfect medium pork chop. Pork is totally fine to eat medium but if you'd like for it to be well done, leave it in the oven for 10-12 minutes.

PAN-ROASTED PORK CHOPS
PICKLED HON SHIMEJI MUSHROOMS
RUTABAGA PURÉE
FRIED KALE AND CHIOGGIA BEET AND SHALLOT SALAD CONT.

MUSHROOMS

1 bunch Hon Shimeji mushrooms, bottoms cut off and broken into individual mushrooms
½ cup cider vinegar
½ cup water
1 t salt

Boil cider vinegar, water and salt for 5 minutes, then pour over mushrooms. Let sit at room temp for 20 minutes and then transfer to refrigerator for at least 2 hours if not overnight

RUTABAGA PURÉE

1 lb peeled and roughly chopped rutabaga
2 cups light chicken stock (no roasted stock here, will change the color and flavor too much)
1 ½ t salt

Bring rutabaga to a boil with chicken stock and salt until fork-tender. Purée in batches in a blender or with a hand blender. Vitamix is the best tool for this job, but you just want the purée to be as silky as possible. Add salt to taste if necessary.

FRIED KALE

1 bunch kale, stemmed, cleaned and torn into pieces
4 T avocado oil
pinch of salt

In a large cast iron bring the avocado oil up over medium-high heat for 3 minutes. When the oil is hot, fry the kale in batches. BE CAREFUL. There is a ton of water in the kale and it will splatter all over, it takes about 12 seconds for it to cook all the way. Remove and place on a sheet tray with a paper towel. Sprinkle with just a touch of salt.

CHIOGGIA BEET SALAD

1 cup beets, shaved thin
in a cross-section
1 shallot shaved thin
1 T apple cider vinegar
2 T extra virgin olive oil
1 T fresh-picked thyme
pinch salt and pepper

Combine all ingredients in a bowl, let sit for 2 hours before serving.

To bring everything together, slice pork chops into three pieces. Divide rutabaga and place in three spots on long plate. Then plate chop pieces. From here, have fun and make the plate beautiful with the pickled shrooms, beet salad and fried kale.

HALF-SMOKED CHICKEN ROASTED AND SMASHED PARSNIPS AND SAUTÉED KALE

(see p 19 in the short ribs recipe for kale instructions)

SERVES 4

CHICKEN

2 small fryer-size chickens
(no more than 3 lbs each)

Make a basic brine of ¼ cup salt to 2 cups water to cover the birds, leave in brine for 24 hours before smoking.

SPICE BLEND MIXED IN A BOWL

3 T salt
1 T cracked black pepper
1 T smoked paprika
½ T paprika
½ T garlic powder
½ T onion powder
1 T dried basil
1 T dried oregano
1 t cayenne
Smoking chips
(I prefer apple, but anything will work)

This is best performed with a heavy Santoku or chef's knife. Split the brined birds down the backbone. Start at the top of the chicken, pick a side of the neck to put your knife on and push through the thin rib bones attaching the backbone to the chicken. Repeat on other side and remove backbone, lay flat with inside of bird facing up.

Slice in dead center through breastbone splitting chicken into two pieces. Pat dry with a towel, then coat in spice rub. Smoke chickens for 4-5 hours at 250-275 °F. More than likely you will need to rotate the birds once or twice during the smoking, as most home smokers have hot spots and cold spots.

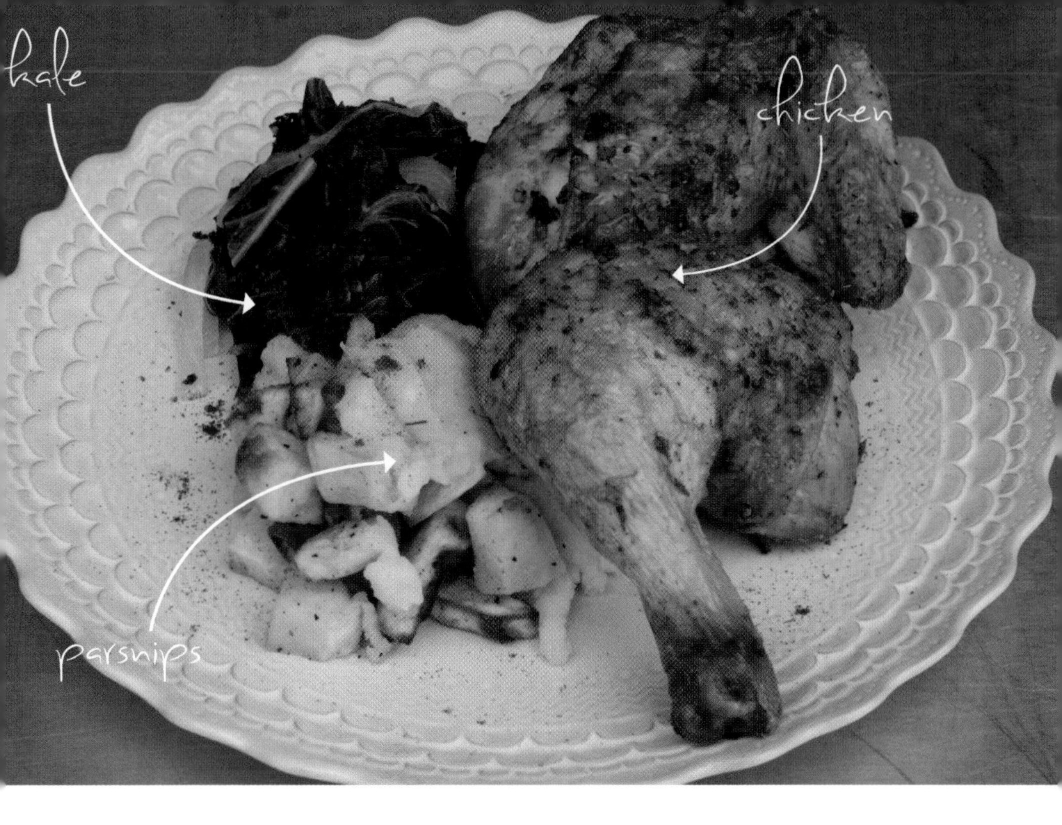

ROASTED AND SMASHED PARSNIPS

1.5 lbs parsnips

¾ cup roasted chicken stock

½ T avocado oil

1 t salt

1 t black pepper

Preheat the oven to 375 ˚F. Peel all parsnips, half can be medium diced (1/2 inch) and tossed in the avocado oil with half the salt and pepper. Place these parsnips on a sheet pan and put in the oven to roast for 35-40 minutes, or until golden brown. Stir them once, about halfway through.

Roughly chopped the other half of the parsnips and put in a pot with chicken stock and enough water to cover. Boil until fork-tender, drain, season, smash, toss with roasted parsnips.

Serve and enjoy.

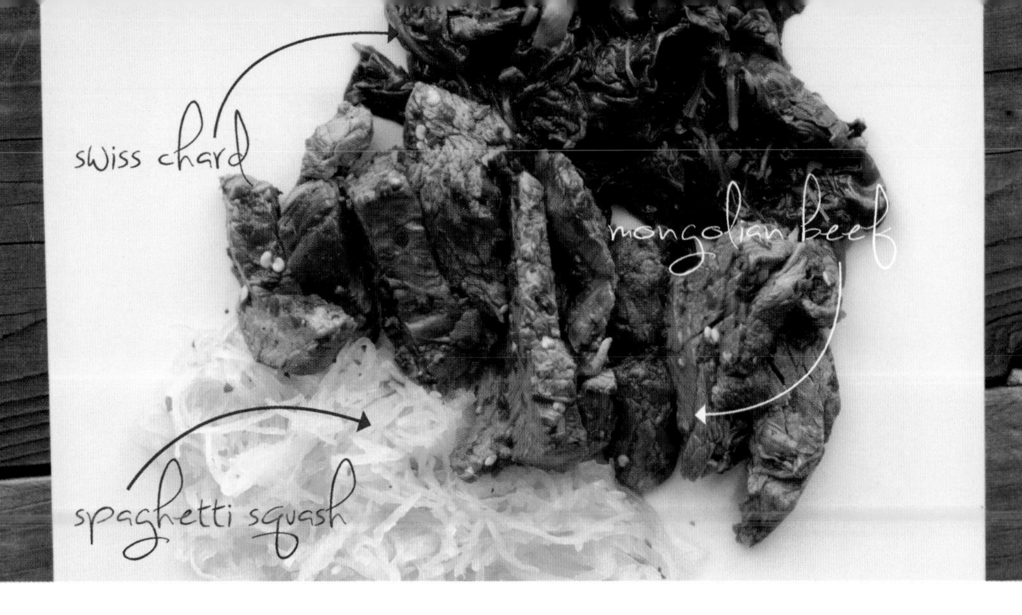

SWISS CHARD

1 bunch Swiss chard, stemmed, chopped and washed
1 small yellow onion, julienned (roughly 1 cup)
1 T avocado oil
½ t salt
½ t black pepper

In a large sauté pan heat the avocado oil over medium-high heat for 3-4 minutes then add the onion and a pinch of salt. Cook on medium for 8-10 minutes, stirring occasionally. You want to be able to get a little color on the onions, but not burn them.

When onions have begun to caramelize, turn heat to high and add Swiss chard along with rest of salt and black pepper.

Stir frequently as the chard cooks quickly. Cook for 2-3 minutes and turn off heat, continue tossing Swiss chard and onions until the Swiss chard is wilted and tender.

Chef's Note:

This is a great new twist on a skirt steak that you might not have tried before. The spaghetti squash method is foolproof for getting it done right every time, making sure you get max yield and the perfect "spaghetti" effect. The Swiss chard is the regular green chard as opposed to the now more common rainbow variety.

MONGOLIAN RED PEPPER BEEF ROASTED SPAGHETTI SQUASH AND SAUTÉED SWISS CHARD

SERVES 4

BEEF

2 lbs skirt steak, trimmed
3 cloves garlic, minced
2 T minced ginger
1 T coconut aminos
2 T honey
½ T salt
½ T black pepper
2 T red chili sauce
(Thai chilies can be simmered in vinegar, salt and garlic, strained and puréed for a homemade version)

Mix all marinade ingredients together and then rub on steak. Let marinate for 1-2 hours at room temp, covered.

This steak is done best over a grill outside, 4-5 minutes per side to medium. If you cook it inside, use a grill plate or a cast iron over medium-high heat at 5 minutes per side. Start cooking the steak when you are warming up the oil for the Swiss chard below.

Let sit for 5 minutes and slice against the grain to serve.

SPAGHETTI SQUASH

1 large spaghetti squash split lengthwise and seeded

With the steak marinating, turn the oven to 375 °F, fill a large baking dish with just under a half-inch of water or so. Place spaghetti squash cut side UP in the dish, toss a couple pinches of salt on the squash and cover with foil. Place in oven for 1 hour.

Remove pan, BE VERY CAREFUL taking foil off. One corner at a time, let cool for about 15 minutes, then using a clean kitchen towel to hold the squash in one hand, scrape the squash with a fork with your other hand. The "spaghetti" will pour into a waiting bowl out of the skin.

From here, with the steak we are just tossing the squash with some salt and olive oil. But you can can turn any traditional spaghetti recipe into a spaghetti-squash version. Have fun.

PAN-ROASTED WILD HALIBUT FENNEL SALAD AND PARSNIPS

SERVES 4

HALIBUT

4 (6) oz pieces halibut
(Get the square shaped pieces, not the long thin ones. They're very hard to work with and cook unevenly.)
2 T avocado oil

Make sure you have a large, seasoned cast iron on hand and begin to warm it over medium-high heat. Have halibut out at room temperature for 20 minutes before cooking. Add oil to pan, when it simmers, pat halibut dry at the last minute, season with salt and then place into pan immediately. Hold the halibut down with the back of your fingers for a count of 15 Mississippi. Then move on to the next piece, starting at 12 o'clock on the pan and finishing at the 9 o'clock position.

Cook for a total of 4-5 minutes, then when golden brown and naturally releasing from pan (don't force it!), flip and cook for 3 minutes on the other side. Keep the heat up the whole time. Make sure you have everything ready before you start, you don't want to walk away and have this undoubtedly expensive fish go to waste.

Let rest for 2 minutes on a paper towel and serve.

FENNEL SALAD

2 bulbs fennel with stalks and fronds removed
1 small yellow onion (¾ cup)
1 Meyer lemon
5 T extra virgin olive oil (the good stuff makes a difference)
1 t salt
1 t black pepper

Remove bottom fifth of fennel bulb, the base root part. Stand up bulb on flat surface you've just made and slice thinly from top to bottom. This will make very pretty full pieces of the bulb. Julienne an onion, toss with fennel, Meyer lemon zest and juice, salt and pepper. Let sit for 30 minutes in the refrigerator then add olive oil. Combine and serve.

PARSNIPS

1.5 lbs parsnips

¾ cup roasted chicken stock

½ T avocado oil

1 t salt

1 t black pepper

Preheat the oven to 375 ˚F.

Peel all parsnips, half can be medium diced (1/2 inch) and tossed in the avocado oil with half the salt and pepper. Place these parsnips on a sheet pan and put in the oven to roast for 35-40 minutes, or until golden brown. Stir them once, about halfway through.

Roughly chopped the other half of the parsnips and put in a pot with chicken stock and enough water to cover. Boil until fork-tender, drain, season, smash, toss with roasted parsnips.

tangelo-turmeric vinaigrette
poached sablefish
black radish
sautéed kale

POACHED SABLEFISH SAUTÉED KALE BLACK RADISH AND TANGELO-TURMERIC VINAIGRETTE

SERVES 4

1.5 lb sablefish (black cod, butterfish)
2 tangelos or tangerines
1 black radish (slightly bigger than a golf ball), julienned
1 bunch kale
1 T fresh turmeric (handle with gloves and only on a very cleanable non-porous surface, this stuff stains)
2/3 cup avocado oil
2 cups vegetable or fish stock to poach fish

You want to get the vinaigrette made and set aside. You can double or triple this recipe and keep it in the fridge for two weeks. The dressing simply makes food come alive, it's just so tasty. The turmeric and tangelos have so much goodness packed into them. The avocado oil is a nice choice here because it doesn't overpower the turmeric and tangelos with its flavor.

Dice the turmeric, zest and then peel the tangelos. Squeeze the leftover peels for their juice and add the zest and juice to the turmeric. Add a pinch of salt and black pepper, then, using a stick blender or a food processor, purée the ingredients while slowly adding the avocado oil. Adjust seasoning to taste, store in refrigerator for at least 2 hours and up to 2 weeks.

Clean the sablefish, removing any bloodlines and portion into 5-6 oz pieces that will be easy to take in and out of the poaching liquid. Aim for a piece about the size and shape of a deck of cards. Bring poaching liquid up to temp over medium-low heat, it should barely be simmering, under 180 °F. Heavily season the liquid so as to taste like sea water.

As the poaching liquid comes up to temp, clean, chop, wash and dry the kale. Sauté over super high heat in a cast iron with just a touch of avocado oil. Hit with a pinch of salt and turn off heat after just 2 minutes. Kale will continue to cook while still in pan. Drop the fish into the liquid and cook for 4 minutes. Remove from liquid and let sit on plate for 4-5 minutes. You can discard liquid and gently break fish apart with a fork.

Place kale on the plate with the shaved black radish, top with poached fish, tangelo slices and vinaigrette.

PEAR AND PROSCIUTTO SALAD

SERVES 4

4 Bosc or Asian pears
8 oz thinly sliced prosciutto
2 T extra virgin olive oil
1 T aged balsamic (if you have the nice stuff, now's the time to use it)
½ t salt
½ t black pepper
1 T basil chiffonade

Quarter, seed and then slice pears. Toss pears with olive oil, salt and pepper. Gently, fold in prosciutto, divide evenly amongst four plates, then drizzle with balsamic and top with basil.

pear
prosciutto

okra
chicken

CHICKEN AND OKRA STEW

SERVES 4

4 cups braised, pulled chicken
(3 lbs chicken thighs covered in chicken stock, with a pinch of salt, pepper, garlic powder and paprika for 3 hours, then cooled and pulled.)
4 cups braising liquid
2 cups Roma tomatoes, roughly chopped
1 cup red bell pepper, chopped
1 cup onion, chopped
2 cups sliced okra
2 T avocado oil
2 t salt
1 t black pepper
2 T chopped fresh parsley

Add avocado oil to a large soup pot and turn to medium-high. Let warm for 2-3 minutes then add onions, peppers, and okra. Use just a pinch of salt and let sauté for 10-15 minutes. Then add tomatoes, another pinch of salt and turn to high, stir often while the tomatoes release all of their water. Cook for 10 minutes then add chicken and raising liquid.

Season to taste and add parsley to serve.

BRAISED AND CRISPY SHORT RIBS WITH ROASTED CAULIFLOWER AND SAUTÉED KALE

SERVES 4

SHORT RIBS

3 lbs bone-off short ribs (once pretty hard to come by, short ribs are now relatively easy to find, brisket is a fine sub if needed)
1 qt beef stock (broth)
2 yellow onion, julienned
1 lb carrots, roughly chopped
1 bay leaf
2 T salt
1 T crushed black pepper
2 T ghee, for crisping later on

Sear seasoned short ribs in large Dutch oven, cook for 5-7 minutes on each side till golden brown. Add onions, carrots, bay leaf and stock. Cover and cook at 275 °F for 10 hours.

Remove and let cool slightly and then pull. From here you can place ghee into a cast iron and fry the pulled short ribs or store the meat to serve later. It is great for scrambles, frittatas, or crisped up and served on a hearty salad.

CAULIFLOWER

1 head of cauliflower
2 t salt
1 t crushed black pepper

Cut up cauliflower and toss in avocado oil, salt and pepper. Roast in a pan in the oven at 375 °F for 16-20 minutes until golden brown and delicious.

KALE

1 bunch kale
Some onion
1 t ghee
pinch of salt
lemon zest (optional)

The kale is super simple. While the short ribs are getting nice and crispy in a pan, add the ghee to another pan, then add the onions and sauté for 2-3 minutes over a medium to high heat. Add in the kale, add a pinch of salt, and toss to finish. You really want the kale to be lightly cooked with this dish. I prefer to add just a touch of lemon zest to my kale when I'm serving it with all of these complicated, rich flavors.

Chef's Note:

This is a great recipe to double or triple to have tons on hand throughout the week for everyone to eat.

BRAISED PULLED PORK
SAUTÉED KALE
ROASTED BABY CARROTS WITH GARLIC

(For the kale, reference recipe on p 19)

SERVES 4

PORK

2 lbs pork shoulder
1 T salt
1 T black pepper
½ T garlic powder
½ T paprika
1 yellow onion sliced
3 cups chicken or pork stock
1 T avocado oil

Cut pork up into 1 inch cubes and rub with the spice blend. Let sit for 30 minutes in a refrigerator. Then in a large Dutch oven, add the avocado oil and turn to medium high. Add onions when oil is heated with a pinch of salt. Cook for 3 minutes then add pork. 8-10 minutes stirring lightly. You want to get a lot of golden brown flavor here and lots of stirring will prevent that.

Add the 3 cups chicken stock. Scrape and deglaze the pan then cover and put into a 250 ˚F oven for 6 hours. Shred and serve with the liquid.

CARROTS

1 ½ lb carrots, either baby carrots peeled and greens trimmed, or large carrots can be subbed and cut batonnet into ¼ inch

4 cloves garlic

3 T avocado oil

1 t salt

½ t black pepper

Preheat oven to 375 °F then peel, chop and clean carrots. Mince garlic by going over each clove once with the blunt side of the knife, then flipping over and chopping your mashed garlic. Add a pinch of salt to the garlic while it's on the cutting bard and go back and forth chopping a few more times.

The salt will pull moisture out of the garlic, almost puréeing it on the board. Toss carrots onto a lipped sheet pan with garlic, oil, salt and pepper. Place in oven in the middle rack.

Roast for 35 minutes, or until tender and golden brown. Toss with chopped fresh parsley for a very vibrant presentation or simply serve as-is.

PLANTAINS

1 cup avocado oil
3 plantains, peeled and cut into
1 ½-inch-thick slices
salt

Warm the avocado oil in a cast iron pan for 6 minutes on medium heat. Using a pair of tongs, place all the plantain slices in the pan starting at the 12 o'clock position and working clockwise so you can keep track of which ones went in first. When they begin to turn golden brown, after about 2 minutes, start again at the 12 o'clock position and flip them over and cook for another 2 minutes. Remove from the pan and set on a sheet pan lined with paper towels. Leave the cast iron pan with the oil on the stovetop and turn the heat down to low.

After the plantains have cooled, about 4 minutes, gently smash them with a small sauté pan to about 1/4 inch thick, pushing straight down. Don't push too hard or they will separate.

Turn the heat under the oil back up to medium and fry the smashed plantains for 2-3 minutes per side. Transfer back to the paper towels and sprinkle liberally with salt. Cool before serving.

CRISPY PORK SHOULDER ROASTED CAULIFLOWER SMASHED AND ROASTED PLANTAINS

SERVES 4

PORK

Whole pork shoulder (2-3 lbs)
2 t salt plus additional for dusting the shoulder
1 t crushed black pepper
2 cups dry white wine, such as Sauvignon Blanc
2 yellow onions, thinly sliced (about 2 cups)
2 to 3 sage leaves
3 cups of chicken stock (you want to make this from scratch or buy the Pete's Paleo chicken bone broth)

Preheat the oven to 375 °F.

Heat a dry large braising pan (ceramic-coated cast iron pan, thick-bottomed Dutch oven, or thick-bottomed soup pot with oven-safe lid) over high heat. Dust the pork shoulder with salt and pepper. Once the pan is super hot, add the pork.

Sear for a total of 6-10 minutes; start checking the color at 6 minutes. When it begins to turn a deep golden brown, add the wine, onions, and sage. Once the meat has browned, after about 6 more minutes, carefully pull the shoulder from the bottom of the pan. Reduce for 10 minutes, then add the stock and salt and reduce for 5 more minutes. Cover and place in the oven.

Cook for 2-2½ hours. Allow to cool for 30 minutes, then pull the meat.

CAULIFLOWER

1 head of cauliflower
2 t salt
1 t crushed black pepper

Cut up cauliflower and toss in avocado oil, salt and pepper. Roast in a pan in the oven at 375 °F for 16-20 minutes until golden brown and delicious.

Chef's Note:

This recipe can apply to any tough cuts of meats like pork shoulder, brisket, leg of lamb, etc. Experiment. Have fun!

BISON SCRAMBLE SAUTÉED KALE AND SMASHED TURNIPS

SERVES 4

2 lbs ground bison
1 cup grated carrot (finest-grated option)
1 lb purple top or hakurei turnips, peeled and roughly chopped
1 bunch kale, stemmed, chopped and washed
1 small onion, julienned (1/2 cup)
2 cups chicken stock, divided
1 t black pepper
1 t garlic powder
1 t dried cilantro
1 t cumin
Salt to taste throughout
2 T ghee (divided)

Add chopped turnips to a soup pot with 1.5 cups chicken stock. Add a pinch of salt and pepper and turn the heat on to medium-high and let simmer until fork-tender, for about 25-30 minutes. This should be the perfect amount of time to pull the rest of the dish together.

Stem, chop and clean kale and set aside. Turn the heat to medium-high over a large cast iron and add 1 T of ghee. When ghee begins to simmer in 3-4 minutes add the ground bison, grated carrot and spice blend. The spices will toast a bit in the pan. Stir frequently for the first 4-5 minutes, then leave on medium to brown for another 8-10 minutes.

While the bison scramble finishes, toss the rest of the ghee into a sauté pan on high, add the onion and a pinch of salt. Cook on high, stirring frequently until soft, 5-6 more minutes, then add the kale. Cook for 3-4 more minutes, and don't season until its finished cooking down as it is easy to over-season a seemingly giant pile of greens.

Fork-mash the turnips, season to taste, serve with kale and bison scramble.

turnips
bison
kale

egg

vegetables and chicken

ROASTED VEGETABLE CHICKEN SOUP WITH A FRIED EGG

SERVES 4

4 cups chopped, roasted squash (yellow in the summer, butternut in the fall, heirloom in the winter)
1 cup roasted mushrooms
1 cup chopped roasted carrots
1 cup leftover chicken, pulled, BBQ, roasted -- anything works
3 cups roasted chicken stock
4 farm eggs
2 T avocado oil
salt and pepper to taste

All vegetables are roasted by tossing lightly in avocado oil, salt and pepper.

Add all roasted vegetables to soup pot with pulled chicken and stock. Let simmer for 20 minutes and season with salt and pepper. In a separate sauté pan, add the avocado oil and fry the eggs over easy in the avocado oil.

Serve on top of a bowl of the soup. Top with some fresh parsley.

Chef's Note:

This recipe is a framework that you should work around and always be remaking. It's a great way to redo breakfast, it gets rid of all the leftovers in your fridge in one delicious soup, and as always, it's just good real food.

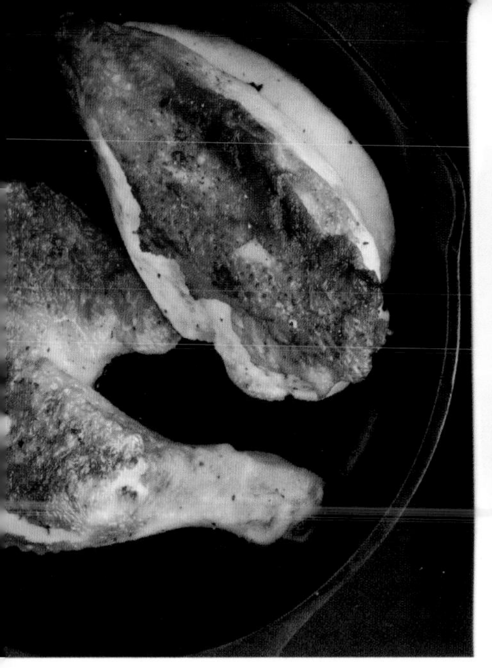

BEETS AND BEET GREENS

2 bunches of medium/baby beets
or 3 large beets with greens
(3 cups of beets and greens)
2 T olive oil
1 shallot, minced
½ cup of chicken or
vegetable stock
salt
pepper

Preheat your oven to 400 °F. Place the whole beets, with greens removed, in a pan with a small amount of water, olive oil, salt and pepper. Cover the pan and let cook for 40 minutes.

Pull the pan out of the oven and immediately chill in an ice bath. After 10 minutes you can pull the beets out, using a paper towel and some gloves, if you want to keep your hands clean. Rub the skin right off and chop the beets into a medium dice.

Clean your beet greens, just like kale or rainbow chard. You are then going to strip the thick part of the vine off, chiffonade them and then wash the greens in water. Now you are ready to make your beets and greens. Lower the oven temperature to 325 °F and finish up your chicken.

While the chicken is in the oven, you can sauté the beet greens with some more ghee, the shallot, and just a touch of salt. Add in the roasted beets, finish with half a cup of chicken stock. Season with salt and pepper to taste.

CAST IRON-BRINED CHICKEN ROASTED BEETS AND SAUTÉED BEET GREENS

SERVES 4

CHICKEN

1 whole chicken
½ cup salt
½ gallon of water
1 bay leaf
3 peppercorns
2 T of apple cider vinegar
1 to 2 T of schmaltz/bacon fat/ghee
salt
pepper

Start by preparing the brine for the chicken. Boil the salt, water, bay leaf, peppercorns and apple cider vinegar all together. Add a cup of ice to chill it down. Then soak the chicken in the brine overnight for 24 hours.

After the chicken has soaked, remove the chicken from the brine and break the chicken down. Debone the breasts and remove the thighs and legs. Keep the thigh and leg meat together. Cover the chicken and let rest at room temperature while you begin to prepare the beets.

Get a cast iron pan out for the chicken. Add just a touch of salt and pepper to the chicken.

Remember you brined it so you do not need to go too heavy on the seasoning for the chicken. Add the schmaltz or bacon grease as the frying oil (ghee would work great as well) into the cast iron. I like to do the legs first, they will take longer to cook because they are a dark meat. Put the thighs and legs in the cast iron pan skin side down. Cook on skin side for 4-6 minutes on medium-high until the skin is a good golden brown. Then flip them over and make room in the pan for your chicken breast.

Put your chicken breast in the pan skin side down. You may want to use an aluminum foil-wrapped brick, the back of your hand, or a pan to weigh down the chicken breasts as they will buckle. Hold them against the cast iron pan until they are good and seared on the skin, this should take about a minute.

Remove the weight and cook the chicken breasts for another 4 minutes until they are golden brown. Flip the breasts over and then place the whole cast iron pan with the chicken into the preheated oven (325 °F) for about 20 minutes.

Pull the chicken out and let it rest for about 7 minutes and then slice and serve with the sautéed beets and greens.

CHICKEN BALLOTINE STUFFED WITH SUNCHOKES, MUSHROOMS, AND BACON FRIED KALE AND ROASTED CARROTS

SERVES 4

CHICKEN

4 skin-on chicken thighs (boned or deboned)

2 cups portobello/shiitake mushrooms

sunchokes

bacon

This dish can be a little complicated. You will have to take the thigh meat and debone the leg. Unless you can find skin on deboned chicken thighs. To debone the thighs, start by splitting the meat on the open side (not the skin side) all the way down to the bone. Then slowly peel around the bone making small slices, butterflying and rolling the bone out of the meat. You want to leave the meat as much intact as possible and be sure not to touch the skin on the other side. The skin is what is going to hold your ballotine together.

Now that you have your chicken deboned, you are going to small dice the mushrooms, sunchokes, and bacon. Add the bacon to the pan and cook. Then, leaving the bacon fat in the pan, add the sunchokes and then add the mushrooms. Make sure the mixture is roasted, caramelized, and seasoned all on its own before you add it into the chicken.

Let the filling mixture cool. Lay each chicken thigh, skin side down, on a piece of plastic wrap and then spoon one tablespoon of the filling into the middle of the chicken thigh. Then, roll the top of the chicken thigh over the filling. Next, roll the chicken thigh tightly in the plastic wrap. The chicken thigh should look like a little sausage. Holding the sides of the roll that you have made, roll and tighten it up even more, then wrap it tightly in aluminum foil. You are going to boil your ballotine so make sure it is nice and tight. Your chicken ballotine should look like a little aluminum popper. From here you are going to boil some poaching water to about 180 °F and then drop the ballotine into the water. Cook the chicken in the water for about 30 minutes.

Pull out your chicken ballotines and immediately put into an ice bath. Preheat your oven to 500 °F. While the chicken is in the ice bath you can get the carrots and kale started.

Once you have finished with prepping the kale and carrots take your ballotines out of the ice-bath. Place them onto a sheet pan, folded side down. Put the sheet with the chicken in the oven for about 9-11 minutes. You are really just browning the outside and warming the insides all the way through since they have already cooked.

Remove the ballotines from the oven and let rest for about 5-6 minutes. Remove the foil and plastic wrap and slice the ballotine very carefully. You are looking for about ¼ to ½ inch slices. Do not try to go too thin, that is when your slices tend to fall apart. You should be able to cut each ballotine into 5 slices. Serve with the fried carrots and kale.

chicken
fried kale & carrots

CHICKEN BALLOTINE STUFFED WITH SUNCHOKES, MUSHROOMS, AND BACON FRIED KALE AND ROASTED CARROTS CONT.

KALE AND CARROTS

3 cups sliced carrots
1 bunch kale
2 T ghee
¼ cup chicken stock
salt

Start by peeling your carrots and slicing them into very thin rings, you want them to cook fast but you also want some crunch to go along with the wilted kale. Then clean and chop your kale. Before adding the carrots to the pan remove your chicken ballotines from the ice bath and put into the oven (refer to the above recipe).

Get a cast iron pan very hot, and add your ghee. Then add in your carrots and a pinch of salt. The carrots will begin cooking. Carrots do take a while to cook so do not move them around, let them get some color and get them nice and pretty. After about 5-6 minutes you can begin to stir them. In about 10 minutes the carrots will be cooked. You can then add your chiffonade cleaned kale. Toss this very well so that the hot oil instantly melts the kale and begins to fry it. Add in a pinch of salt. Toss the kale into the carrots, make sure it is cooked all the way through, about 3-4 minutes of cooking.

Add ¼ cup of chicken stock to the cast iron pan to pull everything together in the pan and serve with the chicken ballotines.

CLASSIC SIMPLE MEATBALLS

SERVES 4

1 ½ lbs grass-fed ground beef
½ onion, small-diced or minced (1/2 cup)
1 T avocado or olive oil
1 t thyme
1 t marjoram
1 t oregano
½ t salt
½ t pepper

Chef's Note:

This is a slightly different version from our video version. Both are good. The important thing to remember with meatballs and Paleo meatballs is that they do not have to have bread or eggs or anything like that to bind them. The meat will just naturally hold together. This is the classic version. You can also do a Persian version and use 1 teaspoon of mint, with some paprika and some garlic and onion powder.

Preheat your oven to 375 °F. Start with the grass-fed ground beef, onion, avocado or olive oil, thyme, marjoram, oregano, salt and pepper. Mix all these ingredients in a bowl.

Make your first meatball at about an ounce and a half. This meatball will be your guide for making the rest. You can use an ice cream scoop to portion out servings. It's always important to measure out portions, so there's enough food for everyone. Plus, everything tastes better because it all cooks in the same amount of time, so you don't have one person with a dry meatball and another person with a raw meatball.

Put your meatballs in the oven. They do not need to cook for more than 9-12 minutes. If you want them to be a little browner you can cook them 8-9 minutes in a 450 °F oven.

This is a great basic meatball recipe. These can also be cooked in the pan if you want to make them a little bit smaller. Make the meatballs a ½ ounce to ¾ of an ounce and brown them directly in the pan. This works if you have something else going in the oven, or if you just want to cook in the pan and do not want to turn the oven on.

BRUSSELS SPROUTS

1 lb whole Brussels sprouts
1 T tallow from short ribs/ghee/avocado oil
1-2 t salt
A touch of black pepper

Preheat your oven to 400 °F. Bring some water to a boil and add in some salt. Add the Brussels sprouts to the boiling water and blanch for 4 minutes. Remove the Brussels sprouts and rinse and shock them with ice water to stop the cooking process. While the Brussels sprouts are cooling down, pick and clean your kale and give it a roughly chopped.

Once cool, toss the blanched Brussels sprouts in avocado oil, ghee, or any type of cooking fat that you want to use. If you have some tallow from the short ribs that were braised, it is really good to toss the Brussels sprouts in. Add the salt and a touch of black pepper. Put the Brussels sprouts onto a sheet tray into the oven until they are golden brown and delicious, which is about 15-20 minutes. I always tell the guys in the kitchen when 5 percent of the pan of Brussels sprouts are burnt then they are perfect. You will not want to do that, but trust me when you get there, you'll understand. It's perfect. Just go all the way, it's worth the extra taste. That's how you get people to say that they like Brussels sprouts when they never liked them before

BRAISED SHORT RIBS SAUTÉED KALE AND ROASTED BRUSSELS SPROUTS

SERVES 4

SHORT RIBS

3 lbs short ribs
3 cups beef stock (or chicken)
3 cups water
1 onion
1 carrot
1 bay leaf
couple of sprigs of thyme
salt
black pepper
avocado oil or ghee

Preheat your oven to 275 °F. Then add salt and pepper to your short ribs, put the short rib into a hot Dutch oven with a little bit of ghee or avocado oil.

Sear the short ribs well on both sides, and then add in your beef broth. Deglaze all the brown stuff off the bottom, add in your vegetables, bay leaf, thyme and water into the Dutch oven. Put the Dutch oven, covered, into the oven and come back in 9 hours.

This is something that is ideally done the night before. Once the veggies are ready, pull the short rib and fry it in a pan with some ghee or bacon fat until it is good and crispy. Almost like a little short rib hash (you can do this with brisket as well).

KALE

1 bunch kale
Some onion
1 t ghee
pinch of salt
lemon zest (optional)

The kale is super simple. While the short ribs are getting nice and crispy in a pan, add the ghee to another pan, then add the onions and sauté for 2-3 minutes over a medium to high heat. Add in the kale, add a pinch of salt, and toss to finish. You really want the kale to be lightly cooked with this dish. Since you have very rich Brussels sprouts and crispy short ribs, you want the kale to be lightly cooked so it shines through and keeps the dish light. I prefer to add just a touch of lemon zest to my kale when I'm serving it with all of these complicated, rich flavors.

PICKLED BEETS

SERVES 4

- 2 cups golden beets
- 1 ½ cups apple cider vinegar
- ½ cup water
- 1 bay leaf
- 3 peppercorns
- 1 T salt

First start by making your pickling liquid. Mix the apple cider vinegar, water, bay leaf, peppercorns and salt and then bring to a boil. Boil the pickling liquid for 15 minutes.

In the meantime peel and slice the beets into wedges and add into a mason jar. Pour the pickling liquid when done over the beets, and let it come to room temperature. Cover the Mason jar, let it sit out for a few days until properly pickled. The length of time you pickle it is up to your tastes -- whatever tastes good to you. Place in the fridge for a few weeks for an awesome condiment that you made yourself. It's delicious, it's good for you, and very easy to make.

GRILLED PEACH AND BACON SALAD WITH CHIVES AND RADISH

SERVES 4

4 ripe peaches
½ lb of pastured bacon
(preferably sugar-free or Pete's Paleo bacon) cut into lardons
¼ cup of chives
1 cup shaved d'avignon radish or breakfast radish
1 shallot, shaved (roughly ¼ cup)
2 T apple cider vinegar
2 T bacon fat (slightly warmer than room temperature)
4 T avocado oil or very light olive oil
salt and pepper to taste

Start by rendering the bacon to get your bacon fat and also to crisp up the bacon lardons. You want to render them until they are 2/3 to 3/4 of the way done, when bacon lardons are almost done, turn off the pan, and let them crisp up in the residual heat. Trust me, it may look like it needs more time but it doesn't.

While the bacon is rendering you can turn the grill on. It is important that the grill is super hot and super clean. You want to have those really pretty grill marks on the peaches, and you want to be able to get them off in one piece. Both of those require a very hot and a very clean grill. Make sure to scrub it down before you use it or while it is heating up, it may be easier to clean.

Now you are going to want to take some high heat oil like avocado oil or an animal fat and rub the grill down, just a very light rubbing of the high heat oil before you add the peaches. Cook the peaches 2-3 minutes per side until they release. You just want to lightly char and get the nice sear marks, and caramelize just the outside of the peach and soften it a bit. They will cook very quickly, then pull them off.

You do not need to add any oil onto the actual peaches, unless you find that it is a little easier to remove with just a light coating of avocado oil. Just toss them in about 1 tablespoon avocado oil and a couple of pinches of salt right before they are about to go on the grill. Do not toss them with the oil and salt head of time, you are going to leech the moisture out of the peaches and you will not get those pretty grill marks, and they will just turn into mush on the grill.

Now you can make the vinaigrette. Add the apple cider vinegar to a blender with the chives, a pinch of salt and a pinch of pepper. Give that a purée in the blender before you add any fat, and then you can slowly drizzle in the bacon fat and the rest of the olive oil or avocado oil, whichever you choose to use. Then add salt and pepper to taste.

Now bring out the bacon, the grilled peaches, the shaved shallot, and the shaved radish. Place everything in a bowl all together, toss with the chive and bacon fat vinaigrette. Serve in a bowl topped with some fresh chives.

chicken
rice
purée

TOMATILLO CILANTRO PURÉE ROASTED CHICKEN AND LIME CAULIFLOWER RICE

SERVES 4

TOMATILLO CILANTRO PURÉE

15 tomatillos, peeled, chopped
1 bunch cilantro, chopped
24 fl oz beef broth
2 T olive oil/coconut oil/ghee
salt to taste

In saucepan add cooking fat, tomatillo and a pinch of salt. Sweat until soft. Add beef broth, bring to boil, then reduce to simmer. Let simmer for 15 minutes. In a blender, add mixture along with cilantro and purée until smooth. Add salt to taste, and serve.

ROASTED CHICKEN

4 chicken thighs, bone-in, skin on
1 pinch sea salt
1 pinch pepper
2 T olive oil/coconut oil/ghee

Heat cooking fat in skillet for 3-4 minutes. Season chicken with salt and pepper. Place chicken in skillet skin side down and sear until nice and golden brown. Flip chicken over and place skillet in oven for 10 minutes or until an internal temp of 150-155 °F has been reached. Remove from oven and let rest for 10 minutes. Chicken will continue cooking while it sits. Ensure the minimum temp is reached; when in doubt, use your meat thermometer.

LIME CAULIFLOWER RICE

1 head cauliflower, grated
1 T ghee
2 T chicken broth
zest of 1 lime
salt to taste

In skillet, heat ghee over medium-high heat. Add grated cauliflower and sauté briefly to soften. Add salt, lime zest and chicken broth. Sauté briefly. Season to taste and serve.

BUTTERNUT SQUASH SOUP

SERVES 6

- 2 butternut squash, peeled, deseeded, diced
- 6 cups beef broth
- 2 T olive oil
- sea salt to taste

In saucepan, add olive oil and squash. Sweat for 5 minutes. Add beef broth and bring to a boil then reduce to simmer. Simmer for 30 minutes. In a blender, purée mixture until smooth. Adjust seasoning with salt to taste, then serve.

TOMATO SOUP

SERVES 4

Two 28 oz cans
San Marzano tomatoes
3 cups chicken broth
1 T apple cider vinegar
2 T olive oil
2 T basil, chopped
sea salt to taste

In saucepan, combine olive oil, a pinch of sea salt and tomatoes. Stir and let simmer for 5 minutes. Add chicken broth and basil. Bring to boil then reduce to simmer. Simmer for 15 minutes. In a blender, purée mixture until smooth. Season to taste with sea salt then serve.

PEA PURÉE, KALE, AND RADISH SALAD

SERVES 4

1 cup fresh picked spring peas
½ cup chicken broth
1 bunch kale, destemmed and torn into shards
1 cup shaved and julienned watermelon radish, black radish and purple radish, split evenly
2 T baby Chinese cedar
1 t salt
½ t black pepper
2 T avocado oil
1 T cider vinegar
1 cup avocado oil for frying kale

Place peas and broth in small saucepan, add a ½ t of salt and turn on high. Boil for 10 minutes and purée. While peas are boiling, slice and dice your radishes and toss in a bowl with 2 T avocado oil, cider vinegar, rest of salt and black pepper. Set radish salad in refrigerator. Place avocado oil in large cast iron and turn on high. When oil hits 325 °F, add kale in batches, and use a fry screen! The kale will pop and shoot oil all over without one. Fry kale for only 10-15 seconds and place on paper towel. Hit kale with just a pinch of salt.

For plating, take a spoonful of pea purée and swipe it along the plate, mound radish salad in the center and dance fried kale and Chinese cedar around plate.

radish
kale
pea purée

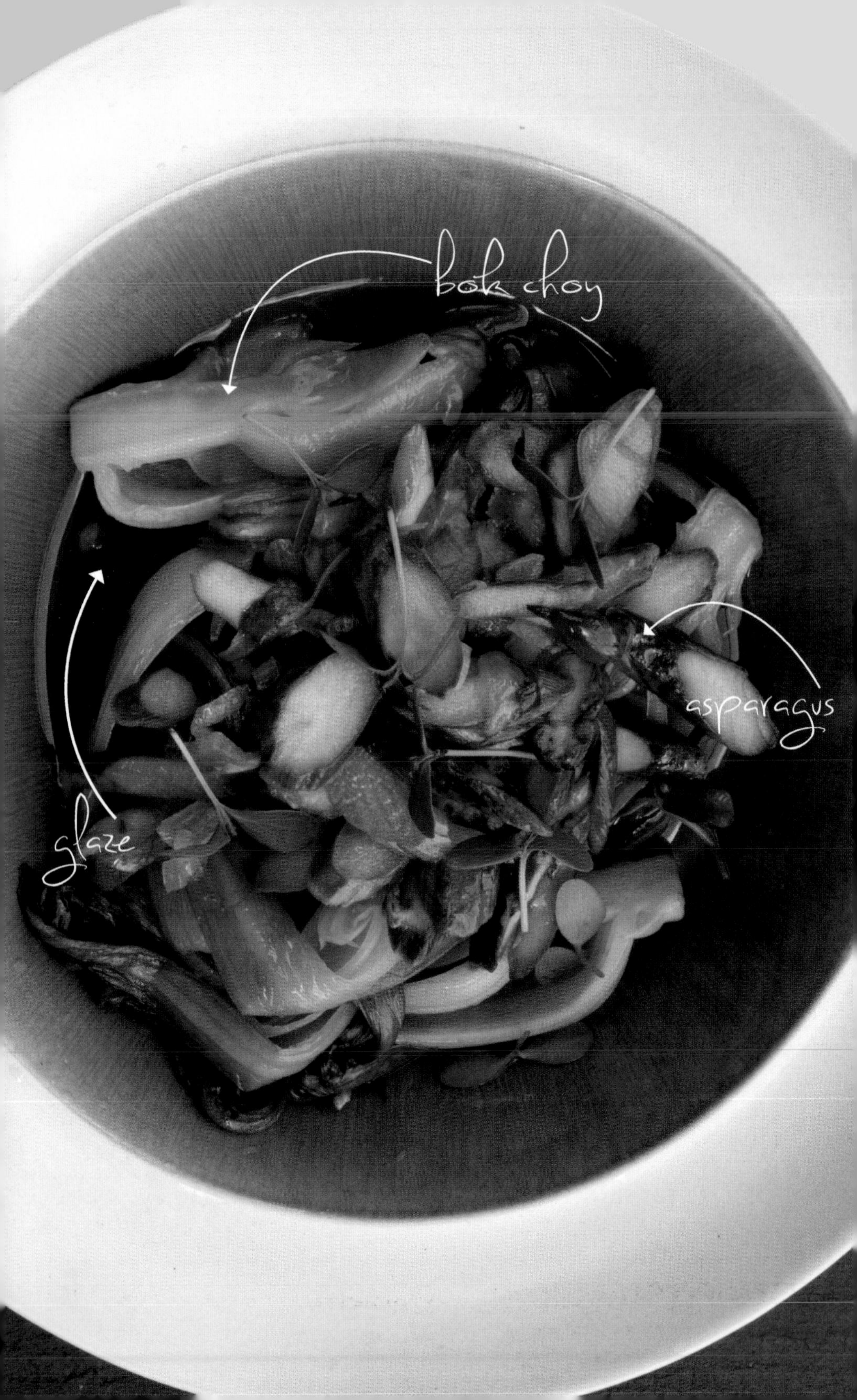
bok choy
glaze
asparagus

BABY BOK CHOY PURPLE ASPARAGUS WITH CHICKEN BROTH GLAZE

SERVES 4

1 bunch purple asparagus, sliced on a thin bias (1 lb)
1 bunch baby bok choy cut in half through the stem (1/2 lb)
½ cup chicken broth
1 t salt, divided in half
1 T ghee
1 t Chinese cedar used as garnish (not necessary, but pretty)

Add ghee to medium sauté pan on medium-high heat, and sauté bok choy for 3-5 minutes, then add ½ t of the salt. Toss gently and sauté for 3 more minutes. Add the asparagus and remaining salt. Again toss gently and sauté for 3 minutes, then add broth and turn heat to high. Once liquid is reduced by half, in about 4 minutes, turn off heat, toss to glaze and serve.

CAST IRON ROASTED KUMQUAT AND SWISS CHARD

SERVES 4

- 1 pint kumquats, sliced (2 cups)
- 2 bunches Swiss chard chiffonade (6 cups)
- 1 T ghee
- ½ cup chicken broth
- 1 t salt, divided in half
- ¼ t black pepper

In a large cast iron, heat the ghee over medium-high heat for about 4 minutes. Add sliced kumquats, and half of the salt. Stir to incorporate and leave it alone for 4 minutes. You want the kumquats to sear on the cast iron and get a good char. When the kumquats get some good color, add the chard on top but still don't stir. Add the remaining salt, black pepper, and then the broth and stir. Cook for 3 minutes on high and serve.

swiss chard
kumquat

snap peas
mushrooms
mint

SNAP PEAS MOREL MUSHROOMS WITH MINT

SERVES 4

1 lb snap peas sliced on a bias
½ lb morel mushrooms, washed, dried and split lengthwise
3 T fresh mint, torn
1 T ghee
½ cup chicken broth
1 t salt

Add ghee to large sauté pan over medium heat. After 4 minutes add the morel plus half the salt. Sautée for 6-7 minutes, stirring only when necessary to keep it from sticking to pan for too long, add snap peas, broth and remaining salt. Cook for 3-4 minutes until broth is reduced by half, turn off heat and add mint. Toss and serve.

PORK BELLY

SERVES 4

2 lbs pork belly
2 cups chicken stock
1 cup hard cider
1 T chili garlic paste
½ cup microgreens including shiso and cilantro
½ T salt

Day before serving:

Rub pork belly with chili paste and salt. Place in shallow baking pan, cover with stock and cider. Cover with foil and cook at 215 °F for 15 hours. Remove from oven and chill overnight. Save liquid.

1 hour before serving, put liquid into small sauce pot and begin to reduce on medium. Set to one side of burner to create convection and gently skim the liquid as film settles on top. Reduce by half until coating the back of a spoon. Slice belly into 1 inch x 3 inch pieces. Turn a large cast iron to medium-high and add pork belly without any additional fat and while pan is still heating up. Roll belly over onto all four sides, cooking 2-4 minutes a side until golden brown and delicious.

Serve two slices per person, coat with the reduced sauce and top with a pinch of micro greens per serving.

SAVORY CAST IRON PANCAKES

SERVES 4

OK, so first and foremost, I took the inspiration for this recipe from Diane Sanfilippo, author of ***Practical Paleo***. She wrote the intro to our book, ***Paleo by Season***, wrote hands-down the best starter guide to Paleo in ***Practical Paleo***, and had a pretty damn good idea with her sweet potato pancakes. However, I was looking to add a more savory flavor and depth to it. So our secret ingredient in these Paleo pancakes is shallots (the onion's pretty little sister you wish you met first).

My sister-in-law made them for us using Diane's recipe last year during Thanksgiving and they were incredible. This weekend I wanted to make them and per usual I don't measure or look at stuff and just kind of winged it. They came out pretty bomb. Feel free to do your own experimenting. It's how you learn and get better as a chef. Also, I made a tasty watermelon salad that was just fresh end-of-summer melon, balsamic reduction, chopped basil, black pepper, salt and some chopped "Dang" coconut chips.

PANCAKES

2 cups small diced sweet potatoes (1 good-sized sweet potato did the trick)
¼ cup minced shallot (1 large shallot)
3 T coconut oil
4 ripe bananas
5 eggs
1 T maple syrup
¼ t cinnamon
1 t baking soda
pinches of salt, as called for
Avocado oil and a well-seasoned cast iron or a non-stick if it makes your knees weak thinking of cooking these in a cast iron.

Heat coconut oil in a medium sauce pot over medium-high heat and add shallots and sweet potatoes. Add a couple pinches of salt, and stir occasionally. By cooking the potato and shallot in a pot instead of sauté pan, it lets the vegetables cook in their own liquid so you don't have to add any extra. When potato is cooked through, in 12-15 minutes, take off heat.

Transfer to narrow bowl for mixing, let stand 10 minutes, then add chopped bananas, maple syrup, cinnamon, baking soda and purée with hand blender. You can use a food processor if you don't have a stick blender. Crack eggs into purée and a couple pinches of salt, purée on low and then turn your cast iron onto medium.

After heating cast iron for 6-8 minutes, add a tablespoon of avocado oil and cook the cakes into 3-4 inch diameter. Like most pancakes, when the edges are firm and there are bubbles throughout, it's time to flip. Then cook for half the amount of time on the other side, roughly 2 minutes. Stack them in a pile as you go. They'll all stay hot and they are good. Real good.

pancakes

bacon maple sauce

SWEET POTATO AND BANANA PANCAKES WITH BACON MAPLE SAUCE

SERVES 4

PANCAKES

4 cups chopped sweet potatoes (roughly 2 medium sweet potatoes)
1 ½ cups chopped bananas (approx. 4 bananas)
12 eggs
½ t cinnamon
½ T salt
½ t baking powder

SAUCE

½ lb sugar-free bacon cut into lardons
½ cup (3 average sized) shallots, thin sliced
½ cup maple syrup

Cover chopped sweet potatoes in water in a small sauce pot and turn to high. Boil potatoes till soft, about 20 minutes. While potatoes are boiling, chop up the bananas and crack the eggs. Mix the bananas with the eggs, cinnamon, baking powder and salt in a tall mixing bowl, with a stick blender, purée all ingredients together and let stand. When potatoes are fork-tender, strain and let air cool for 10 minutes.

While potatoes are cooking, begin to render out the bacon on medium in a cast iron pan, when it is 2/3 of the way cooked add the shallots and stir. Cook on medium for 5-6 minutes then add maple syrup. Leave on low, stirring occasionally the entire time you are cooking the pancakes. It will reduce by 1/3 and will be your perfect sauce.

This, by the way, can be used on just about anything, chicken, pork chops, salmon, Brussels sprouts, a spoon. It's three ingredients and it's really easy, and really tasty.

Now that the sweet potatoes are still warm but not hot, purée them into the egg and banana mixture working in small batches. Add a few spoonfuls of the potato at time. Look for a super fine texture. Using the biggest non-stick pan you have, starting at the 12 o'clock position on the pan on medium-high heat make them about 3 inches each. Cook for about 3 minutes each side, and store in a pile. They will stay warm.

Serve with sliced bananas and topped with the sauce. It is a super-rich, very tasty breakfast that's actually quite good for you. You know, Paleo.

BORSCHT

SERVES 4

2 large fresh beets
4 small fresh Persian cucumbers
1 bunch of scallions
(5-7 individual ones)
1 bunch of Italian parsley
4 hard-boiled eggs
1 lb potatoes (your choice) boiled
1/2 gallon buttermilk or kefir
small container
grass-fed sour cream
salt and little pepper to taste.

Boil the potatoes in a separate pot.

Boil beets until you can stick a knife through them and they are soft. Discard water and let them cool off.

Take a large pot and shred the beets. Then chop the parsley and scallions and add them into the pot.

Chop the cucumbers and add them also in the pot.

Add the sour cream and buttermilk slowly while mixing. If you want the soup "thinner", just add cold water.

Chop the boiled eggs and put them in the soup. (Add a little salt and pepper to taste).

Keep in refrigerator until cold.

Serve with the boiled potatoes on the side (preferably hot). Garnish with parsley.

Chef's Note:

Our dear friend Birute is from Lithuania and we were lucky enough that she shared her family recipe with us. I enjoyed this soup for breakfast and dinner for a few days in order to finish it all up! I loved serving it with hot potatoes with dill and even bacon on the side!

borscht
potatoes

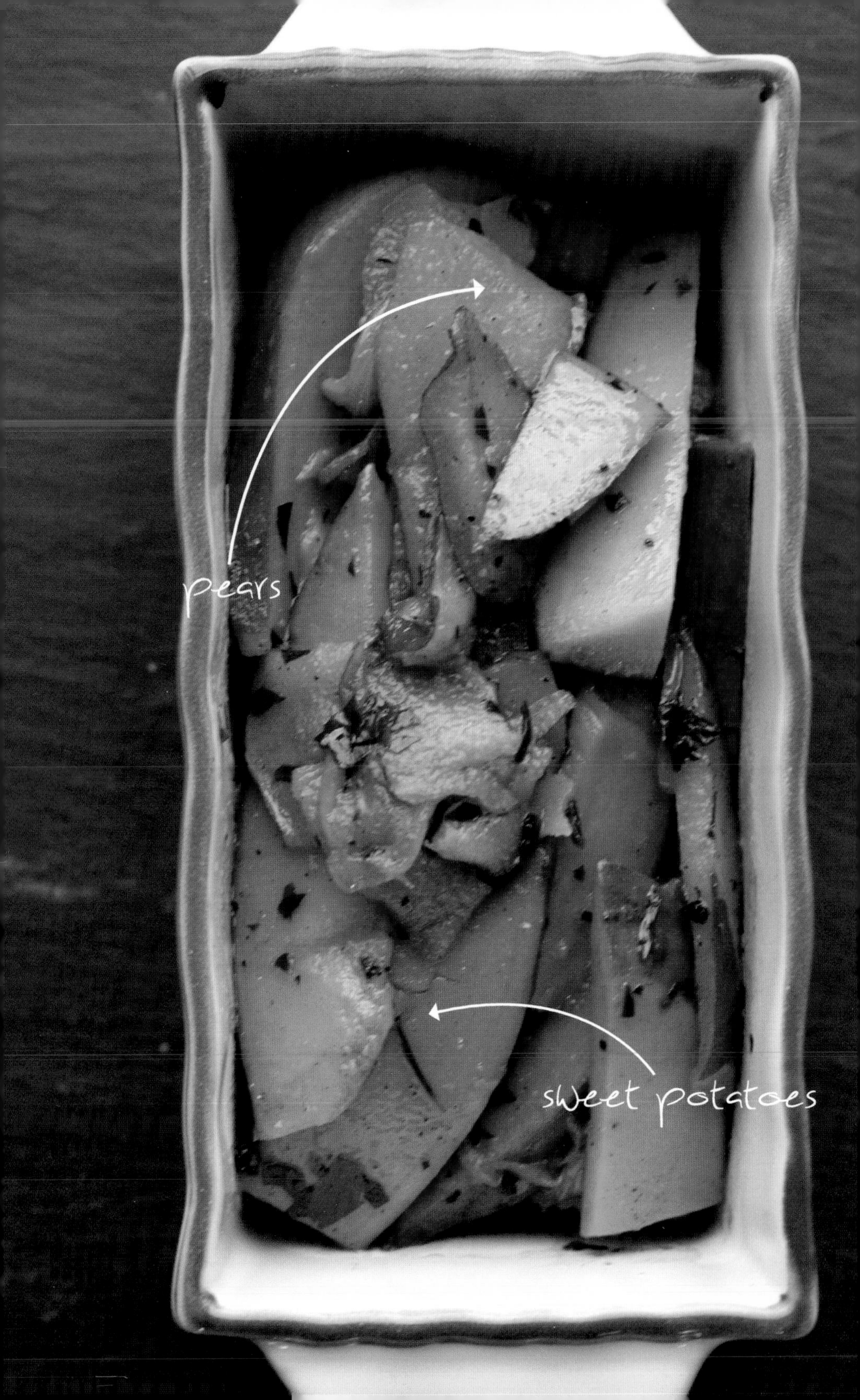
pears
sweet potatoes

SWEET POTATOES AND PEARS STEWED IN GHEE, CLOVES AND BAY LEAF

SERVES 4

4 cups chopped sweet potatoes
2 medium sweet potatoes, sliced in half, then in long strips, like the pears (3 cups)
2 pears, sliced lengthwise to maintain shape (2 cups)
1 yellow onion, julienned (1 cup)
2 T ghee
3 cloves
1 bay leaf
2 t salt
½ cup chicken stock or broth
3 T chopped fresh parsley

Slice all the vegetables, then add half the ghee to a large sauté pan on medium heat. After 3 minutes of heating add onions and a pinch of salt and stir. Cook for 5-7 minutes, until softened, then add pears and another pinch of salt. Cook for 5 minutes then add sweet potatoes, cloves, bay leaf and chicken stock. Cook, stirring occasionally, on medium-high for 12 minutes, season to taste and toss parsley to finish. Remove clove and bay leaf!

BACON BARS

SERVES 4

½ lb sugar-free bacon (like Pete's Paleo bacon) cut into lardons
½ lb almonds toasted
½ lb pecans toasted
½ cup toasted pecans
½ cup chopped dried apricots
1 t cinnamon
1 t salt
½ cup maple syrup
½ cup almond butter
a bit of coconut oil to grease the pan

Render bacon out in a pan until it is crispy. Separate and reserve fat for later on. Combine ingredients in batches, a little of everything each time. Add to a greased baking dish (I use coconut oil) and press the mixture firmly into the pan. Bake at 350 °F for 15-20 minutes. Let cool and then cut to serve. You will have some pieces crumble off that can be used as a bacon Paleo crumble!

SKIRT STEAK ROASTED BROCCOLI AND CUCUMBER, RADISH AND RED ONION SALAD

SERVES 4

- 1.5 lb skirt steak trimmed
- 2 heads broccoli
- 1 cup sliced cucumber
- ½ cup red onion sliced
- ½ cup radish shaved
- ¼ cup red wine vinegar
- 1 T salt divided
- 1 T black pepper divided
- 2 T avocado oil divided

Start by mixing vinegar, few pinches of salt, black pepper, red onion, radish and cucumber together in a bowl. Combine well, cover and leave in the fridge for at least 2 hours before serving.

Season steak with salt and pepper, allow to sit at room temperature for 30 minutes before searing in a cast iron pan, 6 minutes on each side, then into a 375 °F oven for 6 minutes to finish.

While steak is resting, cut broccoli into small florets, toss with avocado oil, a pinch of salt and pepper and roast broccoli for 20 minutes in a 375 °F oven.

Let steak rest for 5 minutes before slicing to serve. Serve radish, cucumber and onion salad cold with the warm steak and hot roasted broccoli

broccoli
red onion
steak
cucumber

INDEX

A

B

C

G

H